My Head Fits Through Y

Let Me Swing Awhile

Wolf, Kevin Martin

To my favourite
Stephen
♡
Wolf

Alien Buddha Press 2019

Table of Contents

Angel

smell like oak barrels old smoke and charred from
inside comes hope
a new dream she smells of peanut butter
after sex she talks in sleep
old dreams forgotten
names written
angels wings
smooth shoulders surrounded
cold steel concrete suffering madness
art is visceral life unfolding beautifully
rust falls from the ceiling of my soul
splintered heavenly glory out of reach
blow to the temples a lump of enlightenment
mix of bad blood good intentions
I was
Outside smoking
pot
when you
came through truly sorry
didn't see you Face to
Face

these bones do not believe my knife is sharp
show me your kerosene veins
will show you the truth of my words drafted by
blood

words turned to stone cannot feed
nations
at the table of the Lord
America

keep a pint of whiskey in my back pocket
secret dreams are filled with nothing but blues sing
out LOUD silent sometimes nations fall
eyes blink abandonment DOLLARS are for
wedding song roses
blacken sunburnt moon someone loves you
ready to die clean immaculate scapegoat
in style soon alive on the edge of a razor
gods tongues never make a sound once there was a
paradigm shift where mothers milk
spilled blood which leads into today's phallic
empire
no longer pagan one god is enough as we all die
alone

this room i sit is flooded full of decaying matter
inside
your mind is hot dreams still cold i dropped my pen
into this muck got lead belly bone black eyed blues
she says fuck yes when entering the room sips
slowly sings softly anything should notice her
dreams movies everyday showing behind clouds of
eyes that are seen staring back
at me as ghosts that move my picture on the wall
want to touch your lotus ⌈SEP⌉Remember good words
died slowly this Sunday morning at first light as
always the way death walks sideways down the
street looks in windows and makes sure you are
watching T. V. worshipping one god microwave
your dinners let kids eat m$ms drink coca-cola
beside pyramids walk to the store which is the
valley of death in the lower 48

SHE

is a secret
dressed in shadow

dust me with
your ashes

broken down
tears
at midnight
i taste you
as the big star
falls west

grinds me to dust
write my name with
desolation in mind

behind the clouds of
eyes staring back as
she writhes languid
her own special
language

her rain
brings
different thunder

angels looking down
on shaky ground

eighteen white horses
covered lightly with soil
called upon angels
and snow

falling thunder gently
these blues
find trouble

pain
uses every
bit of saliva

already tamed
she walked empty
forest naked

oblivion
forgot to put the beer

in the fridge
left my backpack
covered in snow
outside still cold
on the back porch
she reminds me that
Hollywood is always
warm as she's sitting
cooly legs crossed
rubbing each other
scissors on my lap

FALLEN

would sit with you
If could only wake up
from this dream
she laughs as I cough
tries my soul
tells me
she sharpens her teeth
on bones of old lovers
my bones stack neatly
to devour forever
rolls off my tongue
like words of love
words of hate
seem to fall
from the sky
special place
in the middle
of the night
heat and sweat
life does not
forgive much
See her between

rain drops
that have already fallen

IN REMEMBRANCE

When everything hits
at one time in the evening

In remembrance of reading the newspaper
with coffee at table In remembrance of
the hosts salty flesh and red wine blood
some mornings are soft
possibly a radio playing when
there still was diversity in the
background of your mind
that I'm still not used to
being without

In remembrance of my sleepy eyelids
as they fall heavy as a pile of angel's
feathers fall like windblown tobacco
out of your paper towards a solitary
desert that will be shown to you on
TV as an oasis for only the power hungry

A narcissist creed is power and division
looking at the blade in the hand feeling

gap in teeth with black tongue never up
at the sun rising forgetting to listen to the
yellow or golden Finch's song
of joy exuberantly expressing truth
not shown in the reflection of a mirror

In remembrance of being in America i love
to keep a pint of whiskey in my back pocket
her secret dreams filled with nothing but blues
songs sung in streets as i am silent as nations fall
eyes blink and are abandoned when needed most
turned stabbed backs will pay you back

Please do not abandon when needed most
dollar signs wedding songs roses blacken the sun
burnt moon offering as someone loves you in every
town

Sit down always weary souls rest awhile and wait
to come back into style again soon enough to be
tired of a fight ready to die clean scapegoats
on the edge of a razor of god's tongues that never
made a sound

Some point was a whirlwind of flesh am a cosmic
shit with the key to the universe in my pocket

Got lost in the stars
look out to sea it's
the same thing

Let's smoke now we've got the chance
might be a little while before i cross these
oceans of stars again to see you face to face
hear your ramblings kiss you on the cheek
as you kiss me back as my cities burn to
the ground didn't make a sound to walk on
the Moon or cross your valleys bones adding
an edge to my shadow

Close my crucified eyes devout stars on the run

Forgot which lesson of wrath or love to learn first
as i cross the street not between the lines that lay
hoping the cop car that just passed doesn't turn
around as too many movies play behind my lost sad
soul inverted by a small piece of myself that isn't

sure if jaywalking is against the law like coloring
outside the lines as i have a pistol in my pocket

Another car passes and the next one always speeds
up as i step into the street.

YOU DO NOT LOOK LIKE A WOLF TO ME

a guy walked up
after greyhound

touched down in
Pittsburgh
grabbed my seabag
saying that it was his

growled
told him

"You don't look like a Wolf to me mother fucker!"

He let go and walked
went to the other side of the terminal
sat down
stared at the floor

I bought two cups of coffee
later
handed him one

walked away

without saying a word

MUSE'S EXILE

she
was mad
again

at me
wanting to leave

she told me
I wasn't shit
without her

i said
I'm not shit
either way

what's a muse
without the artist ?

The Punisher

knew
I didn't want her to go

she turned around
bent forward
gyrated her hips
slow flower
blooming in orbit
the sun with her
left hand counter clockwise
circles her ass cheek
hypnotic visions

she stand up
crisp attention

I'm holding broken trances

her right hand
she smacks
her other ass cheek
hard

winks
walks out
without a word

ESSENCE

essence
of soul
is molten
glass

poured
through a
platinum
comb

separated
strands
wound around
a crystal
bobbin
wholesale

a new
religion
bleeds
for you
less

i've
never
learned
a
proper
way to
talk

now
see
Blood
in
Words
and
thoughts

we
dance
demons wait
for supper
I wait
for
Rain

she is
a silver
heaven
never felt

she came
to me
moon
on her finger

my lips
dry
eyes
wet beasts
ears
need laughter
from rainbows

deities that walk
the morning
DEW
i praise
my muse

ME

Already Dead

worms and guts
churning madness

eaten by stomach
butterflies turning
into moths as they
exit eden

if only i can
die a poet

make my words true
my words bleed like
a wound my proud
heart will make
things right

til
then

all a show
for death

seek death
only when
the sun
comes up
your ghosts
are not
my heroes
good thing
planes that
drop bombs
lack rearview
mirrors.

lean away
from shadows
looks less
like death
of a Republic
stuck in place
roses to the
people grasping

fleeting moments
to put on graves
that defile my
light.

Can sins be forgiven now my soul
keeps finding holes in my pockets?

need to be able
to taste and devour
what I'm writing if
written in blood and
iron sustenance
might just settle down

Waiting here to speak
in a snowstorm

oddly at ease
truly American

these blue skies are the
last thing that I remember
her kiss her hair in my face

beauty of
it all

death looks at
us in the
Mirror
like a brother

Me

soul color of moldy bread
crust world of hell
heaven to those so
attuned to hear birds
sing cannot
see them

I know supper is ready
as we are out of
Jewish Kings until
Easter rolls around

I HAVE A DEAD SUNFLOWER

in my trash can
your father cannot do much now being dead, not
physically spiritual death is the same thing

now he looks down on us
all father

never trust a skull
without a wolf
that ravens follow
outlaw
words are precise

Golden death
short gasping breath

early every morning
I've got beer in the fridge

as fog rolls glorious
by dews dawn
losing pagan gods

and knowledge
never knowing what
Fea's breasts look like
hitchhike down the road

still hearing the same songs
everyday my lover visits a
gallows pole through prickly
eyed bush crossing the street
to pick up a penny always heads
up pennies that keep you close
and dear to a hearts fire

CAIRN

look at your cairn
meet me in the
morning with hope

official now that i
left six - pack
of bad beer
Under her bed
beside
my stinking boots

covered up with
nag champa
smelly cobra
lifts the veil
see you at sunrise

sage always permeates
her eyes do also
reside soul in back
of my waterfall mind

loins fire up as
bottles clink since
beginning of time

seen you in shadows
for i am a shadow waiting
for the light
there is not
such a thing
as a face no
one knows

i am a bottle of
dust

react to all the wrong
spirits that guide my bones

look you in the eyes
later

these moments
that i forget hungover

every morning
you
remind me
of life

FUCK

Originally from North Carolina
now in the steel city
Everywhere there is trash in the streets
Davidson County NC to Pittsburgh

kind
mind
burns
skin
out of place

wish i had that red house or blue house
Utopian gardens burn bright best thing is this place
or that one

complicated paid for by Kings of pentacles
cards scrolls archaic
dead daydreams smoke you right in front of the
night
forever grateful correcting my grammar daydream
nightmares
used to live a normal life woke up in prison

American felon, ex drug user
anticipated soft scarecrow dreams dystopian

punishment walking willows
worry about what is right or wrong
judge and jury executing drinks at lunch time
went for the biggest one
martinis expensive dinners

retreat sweet face bullets cut through
a chance at life
secrets of earthly treasures high bushy tails rich
with lore of things forgotten
enough for a movie to play behind eyes about this
life I love
how can we start this show?

image of pedigree gotta burn your fire fur that
burns and smells this way of death
really quick succession articles of law and soul
recalling practical sources changing
teaching kids a parallel knowledge ruins sugar
dreams

burns down the high wall of mighty hard living
wonder why ghosts alone in comfort are now
unknown to the average Buddha
walks beside you

a kid at heart
a Samaritan
a refugee with electricity

knowledge held out in front
for all to see

glorious emptiness from streets
lead to the black holes of others
around here graves are stacked
on top of the cold cutting winds

(My Muse) yes this one is about you

When you
think
about me
in the night

i'm Dreaming
of you

standing on the corner
mind's eye
drunkenly
wavering
falling
into
your gaze

my skull shattered
intensely accurate
jig sawed pieces
floating through culverts

away from city lights

above
are eyelids

below
her
eyes are made

of the same colored
glass as a wolf's

pitch black heaven

one mind together
celestial bodies
awaken
brightly
boldly
brazen

right now
my neck has
railroad tracks
covering the
distance of
my hairline

sometimes
need to
put a foot on
the floor to
keep the room

from spinning

new found
metal ritual
watching
shivering dead
spinal dance
carnivals that
bring dirt
loss of light
head straightened
recovery
walks around
looking for less
suffering
hating the least
loving the mist
that the night
falls into at Sunset

there are bits of bone
viscera in my hair

this hibiscus

cured my sleep
apnea

later causing
a stutter

hurricanes
prolapsed

bones sharpened
stainless

burlap
for a wedding dress

white as rain
for a Woman
will never rust

WOUNDS TIME AND HEALING

want to hear you whispering in my ear speaking in
tongues while putting roses on my grave.

Wounds Time and Healing

Bite my lip
tastes of iron
chew my
tongue
to meat
so my words
will mean
something later
my tortured
soul waits
for dust to
settle
mirage
see myself clearly
through eyes made
of glass surviving
heat of today

as angels follow
beauty
and glory
that burnt wings
during the fall
of man
just a little
out of reach
a spectacle viewed
in Heaven from dust
all the same to her
a yellow flower
picked at the last
minute in haste
she accepted
my love
this moment
meant nothing
she recognized
desperation
cool in the morning
sun rising
turned around
smoking a cigarette

while the sun
burned last nights
accumulation of
thoughts and foggy dreams..

FELLA

born to die
born here all of us were
Welcome to your death feast
of flesh or souls snaky noodles
worms a peach or a pig a man
needs to eat grow up big
strong Welcome home prodigal
son be prepared for a toy gun
before a real death by iron
wander gentle plains keeping
her head up she watches me
Hang as we both died inside
our gentle hearts living on at dawn
a fresh hell follows me everywhere

Fragile

male ego
chipped a
tooth

nibbling

on her
glass neck

Winter Wind

sidewalks
taste tears
from my
brainpan
never fall
straight down
count
rain drops
in Babylon
where I am
shaman

SHADOW

corner of my eye
fleeting madness
saw her standing
holding snakes
by rainbow colored tails
the dark cannot hide
when i cannot see her
my soul writhes in agony
beside a metal staircase
there are scratches made
by my belt buckle almost
was not good enough

city wiped sweat stains
across windshield am old
like the road the bridge
over there with mossy lips
believes in a kiss with winds
that shape breath she looked
sad this room has oval eyes

incongruity of totality
some wear me better than
others

fall asleep in antique
rocking chairs
am no longer
chasing the dying

of the light
pushing too hard
burning out was good enough

FEAR IS A CHECK ENGINE LIGHT

fear for some
is the check
engine light

short breath a gasp away

from gasoline fumes

sitting on the side of soft

shouldered yellow lines

can still see your outline

slowly walking away

words draining hope

cannot see her

soul in agony

on the floor

beside a metal staircase

there are scratches

made by my belt buckle

friction enough to burn

Bridges

city wiped sweat stains

across windshields i am

old like the road

rusty water under

Bridges

with mossy lips that shape breath

this room has oval eyes

some incongruity of totality

only some wear it well

others

fall asleep

in antique

rocking chairs

Banks of the river from where i was from have
drowned me several times
her kiss was rock and roll dancing short skirt that
never apologized and didn't have to yell
i yell timber as she's used to big wood promised

in my youth gotten rid of letters of love haven't told
anyone

remember every word said about the first and best
of days
secrecy i kept her fire alive she mined my
diamonds sped out
towards the border as i still ramble mind this ain't
no fucking
game with wishes never good enough in the night
you cannot see
progress until dawn light my words are still golden
laying on the ground
never gave up
on the sun

i was never good with words unless on the run
bleeding temples

blessings that still keep my pace as justice never
rests
my right eye is swollen and seen too much broken
flesh and bone

HEADACHES

future pains never listen
spells dance islands await
incantations predicted
outside my window
an angry god or woman
dancing naked
shame in the colonial sense
dismissed
bloody in streets
my hands are clean
grass behind my tombstone is not
a mountain left to climb
my illness provides curb service
voices shallow eyes look
waiting whispers on nibbles
promises in a dark room
the light startles scurrying
beasts all of us fear punishment
i still love you after
failed suicide attempts
crucified ideals
slow vesper services in the

Apocalypse
arch angels hoarse voices
no longer carried by the sunrise
tears fall taste fire not salt
a cold-water flat dream from
years ago burns away forgotten

Will you do this for me? Sacrifice passing the
shallow euphoric
nightmare stage different lenses

THE OLD MAN

throws rich man's words
far over my head

drowns in the
lushness of old sad songs

antique wooden rocking
chair by a window

coffee cups stained black
burnt with money's friends

i got blues
in my cups
taste hope
at night

the moon always shines
through my window
twinkles in her eyes

sees your shadow
wash hands
of blood
to shake later

WINCHESTER 12 GAUGE

my
family's
shotgun
passed down
from
generation
to generation
was made
of silver
scrollwork
iron and
fire
to my
young
eyes

shot
projectiles
smooth
as
glass

i
remember
paw-paw
talking about
JC Higgins
even though
Sears and
Roebuck
had taken
over
twenty years
before
he could
transition into
how
his Ted Williams
12-gauge pump
was smart marketing
as he leveled
and fired
flawlessly
the mistletoe
fell
in a perfect

bundle
as
intended
every man
in
our family
seemed to
have a gift

could always
hit anything
that was
within range
i
never saw
my grandfather
ever miss
anything he
aimed at
he believed that
every man
should own
one shotgun
one rifle and

one pistol
he
preferred
revolvers
and he
never
pointed
a weapon
at any
living
thing after
the second
world war

DREAMS OF PINS AND NEEDLES

last night
flash of blood inside
cylinder before dropping
hammer down cold sweats
used to be dry sheets
tossing turning old day
dreams

hard to come by authentic ones
cold rusty sinew veins aches deviant dominating
conversation
a new glass in hand raised toward

New Year

new me believing in her myth again

there are always other applicants waiting
happens next i'm sorry no one understands
her love and spark was the last vengeance marching

arriving later after sunset fire on chest my muse
imitates
road construction bridge building bong hits
scorching my throat
downtown wearing a cross of the advocate in
bronze leather
strapped heart my chest is brown two rattlesnake
vertebrae intertwined
joshua
tree thorns taste pierced scapegoat
heart before

i smelled
her perfume or blood l
look into the poor begonias appetite
waiting for tastes to ferment after waking hungover
she realized that she had left her house
without her chapstick

THE UNDERGROUND

abandoned worn
industrial relic
momentary solitude
years ago squatted here
cavernous nights
freight trains
Norfolk Southern sound
riding the rails of your heart
straight through until breaking

dark red waning gibbous moon
top of a maintenance ladder
four shooting stars
dreams of youth
remember the moment
mental illness hiding
slowly reacting
crystal sheathed soul

lies told to keep children in bed
never lied about the night
eyes that follow remember giving up

telling my fifth-grade teacher
going to ride rails
greatest HOBO

Mother Teresa
pittance paper comfort
every town handwritten intentions
pocket watch and chain
hellbent coping mechanisms
self-soothing behavior
rent the veil of childhood

SEEK DEATH

seek death   lean away
only when   from shadows
the sun   looks less
comes up   like death
your ghosts   of a Republic
are not   stuck in place
my heroes   roses to the
good thing   people grasping
planes that   fleeting moments
drop bombs   to put on graves
lack rearview   that defile my
mirrors.   light.

Can sins be forgiven now my soul
keeps finding holes in my pockets?

X-RAY

found out today through an X-RAY
i have spiders and webs in my head
they feed on dreams look like
technicolor pinwheels

party hard on my soft tissues
eat rainbow dreams voice is like
a bat's sonar that taints images of
ghost dust glitter expressions you feel
laugh out loud

tell me my fortune on the street uninhabited vacant
cool dreams that
fall apart slowly my back needs to get
stronger to look for this American
Dream by my bedside safe with
great expectations

nights howl await fire in the old way
sacrifice for the right reasons

this time as i hear gunshots outside
fireworks bring in the new revolutions
chains rattle one last time in the
middle of the night each step walk as
candles flicker still hear explosions in
the back of my mind a northbound train
to carry you over your hump piggyback

if need be as i dream of my muse

behind these American prison bars i am
a young wolf that peers into darkness

REHAB

Last time I was in rehab
there was a guy in the lower bunk on the opposite
wall from me. Every morning at 5:00 am when
retrieved from vivid dreams caused by withdrawal
in a restless night, he would always say "hey Wolf,
did you get the license plate number of that bus that
hit me?" "I hope you kicked the dog that shit in my
mouth."

I'M NOT SICK ANYMORE

thanks for not asking

sitting

across

arm's length

smiling

in her own way

she
said

free
your
mind
I can
see your
old ghosts
flying out

returning
like
wasps
to a nest

only dream now when sober ghosts left grizzled
impressions as I'm now in low cotton as I'll get
what's mine and pure shadows of pines outside
besides letting her get what she wants leads to
smoky cobalt pearls resembling tombstones that
still could be something more in the middle of the
night

always turning her to desired position always
looking into her eyes floods room with light
hunched haunched sometimes she looks away my
feet on floor for stability as i grab her below elbows
her arms held back her hands cashmere opened
graceful gestures ass up i sink and pull back
ungently urgent moans that never refused to echo in
behind my eyes that echo still a cavernous void
recently devoid of old ghosts resonance with
markings left on my walls

now i need her more than ever it's been over a year
as her smell remains in rooms on fire now over my
sickness thank you for never asking my ailment
was basic human neglect of a heart on a sleeve that
never figured out how to build ramparts or turn a
cheek when she decided to not stay a shadow
anymore as I always fail to turn the other cheek

she only reaches out when waking up from
hangover and depression laying thick like her
tongue lays languid side of cheek barely able to talk
she calls me after last night sitting beside and
laying with different men I'm still on her mind at
the bar i used to drink at always alone when the sun
comes up and shines on my desolation

MY MUSE

muse with moon eyes

chases butterflies during the day

moths by night

following rainbows

tied a ribbon around my finger

her stories give me life

our souls sit back to back

y'all like sins companion

drunkard tongue is good

for my mind to find courage

a fool for every fool

My tears burn

glass eyed focus glancing

your direction pieces of puzzles

dancing out of reach are idle idealist

Hating this fucking job i do

chasing rainbows over ridges and hills and slums
sins and souls jump from bridges over weeds of the
side of the turn fork where my lady thinks I did
wrong as she's finally in love as my ax and one
hour of sinking sunlight breaking trail with little
bits of coinage and no cash In my hand everything
is shit and living for tonight right now with hopeful
embraces future sun kisses on my cheek

feel
your
ghost
breathing
on

my neck
the real truth
laid down
for
ever
my truth
is
forbidden
knowledge
led by forbidden nibbles
on skin made for that purpose
to be consumed
nature a soul that burns
antique sand of gods dust choking
the lungs of antique brazen idol
the look of a lioness, a bunny, a fox a vixen licking
blood from..
Whether you save me or not my ghost and shadow
hid a long time ago in the hills behind your green
eyes the eventual mania nibbles behind an ear that
equals
tingling heaven

lost
you
for
a smile

another
stranger

intends
on
blocking
shadows

never trusting
others
apologizing
shallow breath

more than i can
prove waking up
on the ground under
dew and morning
light red and foxy
red

delights
dressed
as
what
you
hate
apologize for
my lies

they are more than I can prove

BURNT SAGE AGAIN

Keep on
falling down

mirrored

kin

susceptible
to old ways of
death
allowed to grow
hating oneself
leads to hate shared
hold out that the possibility
of making it to an age-old death
depends on location and who
around holds onto ages old
racist ideology

belief in a false
state

one
of

only skin-deep differences
different cultural standards

bulky and stationed in hate

forgotten charm of the street,
these forgotten soul fewer walking dead
show up to only take life as the rest
of "We the People" are busy
burying our dead in soiled clothes

the other offended stand ready to protect

the
way
and say
of the gun
held tight to eons
of
fewer
plow shares

mainly swords
to pray
at the temples of Solomon
without hand written folded up
words for gods ears alone slipped
through the cracks of mortal mortar

now blood red flowing down America's
path to the Red Sea contribution

opium is the newest reborn old god
before was bullets scattered through the flesh of
fallen angels

when do we wake up from this side of the
American Dream?

MAN made violence? It's just TVs and blues? A
shot poured out red on the ground? Everyday! This
horror played out on in the patches of youth or old
white men left unsupervised? Played out in the
brain pans of waning empathy that needs to kill
more than is needed to survive to eat to fuck!

i smoke sage again in an altar with tobacco and
spilt blood

gunshots that wash my neighbors windows and
skulls are heard through early morning sirens

i pray on my hill in solitude even I cannot keep my
thoughts to myself as they are close to my heart, my
pilgrimage is towards the holy land that is a heart
reaching out with strength and valor
amidst our continual waging of wars

NEVER BEEN TOO PROUD

i will flip you over and adjust you
accordingly, gravity or the sunset
is payback for words thrown over my
shoulder yesterday morning before i knew what
was going on with this hangover. She said, "it's all
about the next line". I'm not sure if she's talking
about drugs or words but i do know that my time is
imaginary youthful dreams and my tone is
redundant falling asleep every night with words left
unsaid and blood on my tongue. Destiny and her
dogmen eat the flesh of the night to spit up the
sunrise that saw you heading this way. words left
unsaid are a mountain range. these mountains take
up all of my wasted time the sunsets in such a hurry
as we forget each other by dawn
told me in the morning
this was her most
favorite part of my
soul

only heaven can be further away
from me than you are right now

let me ask you something
you think you can buy
salvation
forgiveness
love
comfort?

appearances are nightmares
what's important is inside

soft and gooey bits
emotions molded by
touch

openings to a graveyard
love letters are always
written on tombstones

wedding song death marches
human born cicada molt
shells of husks of people glistening in the corner

of your eye beside a church
long ago burnt down effigy

I've seen
her in action
do not doubt
her movements
intentions
lie down on her
alter the planets
alignment open cosmos
split down the middle
thank god you are here
I'll keep you wet in the
desert gaze i seek your
shelter as only remembered
are good times looking back
over shoulders at pillars of
salt and brimstone

Keep talking
i said to her
looked deep
told me

everything
i
needed to hear
she said
who gives a fuck
smoke your cigar

my world where
words like lightning
bring thunder
luck means
more patience

count the seconds
minutes

i
wait to haunt your ghost
you light candles in the
rain to gods that ignore
good intentions
too honest
i
find mortality more fitting

cicadas in my ears a spark
inside I'll get to you in a second
trust me as we pick each other's
brains might stray from a normal
Life

where everyone looks at you sideways

She said
don't you already do
whatever you want?
You
son
of a
bitch!
everything is real to not have to
miss the taste of you a heart
black
and
blue

i
Live in the
corner

Where
You cut your eyes
Sideways

Working
Your
Tail
Off

Tax free
In North Carolina

Just trying
To get
By

This mountain is my
Home

i was face to face with my sad old tunes
i was face to face with your sad old blues

In
My
Mind you
Were everything

In
My
Mind we're
Hungry
For you blues
That meant something
A long time ago

Since i have
Risen

As the sun
And space and time
Which digs my grave

Fashions my crown

With perfume

i will rise

There is a
loaded
Gun

There is a dusty road
for you
that cries
out loud

Waits
around

Like the mud in a river

HANDWRITTEN HEART

hold

my

hand

written

heart

with

letters

in the

mail

shows

how

much

I've

missed

your

words

alive

alone

ears
that
listen
To
your
distress

FALLING DOWN

again and again
watching her dance
ebb and wane pyroclastic
flow
waxing eloquently
soft caresses
kisses start
with stigmata
wrists taunt
her neck is
lean swan bent
forward leaning
as lovers a long time ago
enact vengeance on each other
taught destinies from birth
conquering souls fiery boundaries
second nature is entwined

fallen angels
tend to burn
together

DROWNING

in thought,
crispy
electrified
visions
as i
close my
tired
eyes
again.

Time
goes by,
she's
always
far
away,
left with
crystal
and glass
shrapnel
hearts, an
obsidian

love
in the
broken
hourglass streets

SNARL

what's
the point

showing your
teeth to others

for
your
own
contemptment

your
own
satisfaction

i
will snarl
incisor
showing

i'm
not scared
or fearful
wolf

smell of
sandalwood
llang
llang

walking
down

railroad tracks

hoping when I get home that in the mail are my
Arby's Hardee's Carl Jr's Pizza Hut promotions and
coupons for direct T.V. Time Warner Cable that is
extremely important so i can be fed and entertained
like everyone else that believes in discounts and
saving money by not having to think for yourself,
we will do the thinking for you i promise you like
everyone else that believes in everyone else....

only matter
to the angel
that collects them
at the bottom
of heaven

STILL ALIVE

alone again
blood waterfall
tears that follow
the Moon and Sun
rising in vein
for the last time

PAYPHONES AND QUARTERS

i
still
remember

pay
phones
and
quarters

meeting
drug dealers
on
corners

i
shiver
and
shake

violently
in my
past

life

sweating
profusely

i
remember
that last quarter
cost me a dollar

almost cost me everything
that I had left when the
county sheriff pulled in
and stopped

touch tones in left ear
now dial tones that match
the beat of my heart

ringing and ringing

i
know he is still there i can smell
him from afar as the radio of

enforced freedom cackles in
his ear breaks like a wave in mine

my connect answers the phone
which startles me and almost
dropped the receiver the
phones cord makes bending
metallic sounds that can be
heard on the other end

that can be heard in Heaven

i
tell my man
that I need to talk
a minute

he said why are you calling
from a payphone?

told him a lie
that my ol lady was being a bitch
smashed my cell phone

wasn't ready to leave quite yet
placed my order which was accepted

half an elbow of blow
a little elephants ear is
what it reminded me of
could see it behind my
eyelids

silence on the other end
he hung up on me as I'm
waiting and waiting for
Davidson County's finest
mother fucker to drive away

i
drop a quarter in and call my
brother who even though at two
in the morning I've woken him up
talks to me and understands
my situation as I lean forward
to adjust the Glock 21 45acp
safety to vengeance as there is
always one in the chamber as

my champion of Justice has had
enough of my laughter and gravel
pops as he pulls away empty blue
lights disappear and i tell my brother
goodnight hang up and pull out my
cell phone to let my dude know that
I'm on my way and I'll meet him at the
spot in thirty minutes.

HUNGER

i
will
eat
you too.
surviving
gnawing
bones
and glass
spitting
out gristle
even the griss
in front
of me
can be
regurgitated

repeated again

until satisfied
reminding me
i have no money
or fancy clothes

yet
i
am

rumbly
tumbly
bones

crashing
breaking

waves

moonshine

your
mind

prefers
heart beats
complexity
i could never
afford

i
will take
what i
can get

or left
with

no difference between

no need to worry
about the fairytale

i remember
the old man
rummaging
behind the bar
where i worked
he was in the alley
between us and heaven
he was looking for hell

he was old
ornery

checking
empty
beer
bottles
and
liquor bottles

scarce scant amounts evaporates

bottles of different colors and sizes stacked neatly
outside
same cartons
that were delivered
last week
now filled with skulls

10 cents
a piece

waiting to be cashed in
dutifully on return

i
was taking out the trash
walking out the back door

heard the explosions like gunfire

instead of putting the bottles
back neatly, he was smashing
the ones
that were completely empty
muttering to himself
why straighten up now?

putting back the bottles that had
an unswigged corner
after re swigging
backwash and strangers kindness courtesy or
neglect
are the same illusion
in the night

he broke 285 bottles out of 350

we were both thinking

about dreams

both
realizing

the same
thing
at a
young age

i
still
cherish
that
Wasted
Time and
Prayers

no one here owes

You

A
Mother

Fucking
Thing!

i
could have stopped him
from
breaking bottles

it was an act
out of
my
pay grade and above my morality god stood
still

didn't want
to steal
joy
he had left

i did get paid
cash

to
sweep up

collateral damage

less confrontational

always
buy
you
a drink
if i knew
that it
would
change
the world

i
can assure
with 100%

certainty

i
would drink
it myself

longing
for
your
noose

i await
your stubborn
American
ways

WHISPERING PINES

Clear Skies

Gibbous
 Orb
chasing
Mars
tonight
after
Venus
dazzling
sunset
appearance

beauty
always
brings
Titans

queen
of
heaven
is

now
tired
asleep

Mars
out
shines
his
Greek
celestial
brother

smells
of
rare
antiquity

papyrus
mold
replaces

moss
and
lichen

replaces
every
smell

except
for
this
Wolf
perpetually
hungry
On
these
nights

story
after
11

Right
now
at
2: 30

the
wind
has
died

eerily
and
cleanly

with
out
a
trace

i
put
my
knife

securely
back
In
it's
home

on
my
belt

i
will
not
live
in
fear

tonight

I
will
burn
smudge
sage
not a good night to
HOWL even if beckoned

i will
sleep with the lights on.

if
at
all

gravel
pops
in
the
distance

hum
of
a
small
light
truck

down
shifting

wheels
rubbery
pinched
sound

texture
when
turning

then
more
gravel

I've
awaited
this
arrival

I've
tasted

wind
death

Never in a dream

last
time
i
was
facing
a
different
direction
2: 30
PM

A lifetime ago

Tasted
Sweeter
than
now

i
hear
mild
squeal

Familiar
sounds

small
creak
truck
settling
stopping

engine dying
doors opening
and shutting

nothing
else

i
wait

no
sound
at all

i
feel
numb

not
in
the
usual
way

there's
emotion
there
it's
well
contained

walk to the front

I'm by myself
except
moon shadow
on a shit ton of
Eastern Pine

Cedar mixed in

Ridgeline
opposite
direction
of a
cat-fish
pond

pay to fish

if you catch
the best biggest
one that night
win money
enter ya in the
drawing for a
Mossberg 12.ga
to be given away
weekend before
the next turkey shoot

Ridgeline
East
towards
the
Heart
of a
countries
and county's
Oldest
mountain
range
that from
here looks
deceptively
close
is
burning
glowing
orange
slightly red
i listen closer hoping
to hear the sounds of
drums and chanting

Hoping and
Believing

Believing in my
headache
and pain
finally has a future
Mars dances
on Earth tonight
before Apollo
chariot
sky crossing

i hear the echoes now of men's idle
conversation proud of the fire built
Vulcan still lies dormant
in his mountain tomb alone
i can see
clearly
where
The Wind
deposited
smell of
pine needles

burning fills
the gaps
colors flicker
across dark
mountains
then disappear
quickly in
the same dance

memory
and dreams
eyes start to open
visions disperse like
fog in the early morning
struggling sun rise
gone before
eyes fully opened
or equipped

pine needles
will
return again
and
fall

A
dignified
death
before cessation
or drought
of my tears
that will only
affect the exact
spot where i lay

1998

her soul i never saw tingling

exuberantly flashing bit by bit by bit
i was upside down flying on words
as serene oceans calm as any man
that has ever found justice or love
if any narrow freedom breathes deeply
champagne aromas pleasing to the touch
trickery on my eyes for I've seen too much Virgin
wool slaughtered under young blades of fiery lust
let me
tell you of resurrection and the proof of
existence crushing grapes to wine
that only ravens or crows will drink.
(1998)

NAPKIN

poem
written
on
a
napkin

The
bartender
threw
It
away

it
was
the
right
thing
to
do

STUTTER

only
stutter

when i
know

what
i.am

talking
about

never
mince
words
that
others
can
turn
to
stone

i
will
be
here
when
the

good
Lord

comes

i
am
here
for
the taking

come get your wolf
Mother Fucker

i

will

and

shall

be

waiting

DAVIDSON COUNTY JAIL

haven't eaten since yesterday tossed to dogs by pigs
flashing lights expose you to everything
inappropriate
first glance sleep with lights on teardrops rise
toward horizons where there is a message in a
bottle waiting for you when you get out of
purgatory healthy clean wings where there was
once smooth shoulders behind cinder block walls
and screened phone calls

rest and take bird baths in cells last time i was
locked up my cell had a million dollar's worth of
bond in a small-town trap off county one of us
always sleeping on the floor

i was in the top bunk as everyone stays up all night
as some sing i read and put my sheet up when I
need to shit the only privacy you get find out who
wins playing poker on aluminum tables and seats
staring contests especially at chow i tap the table
with metallic ring twice before i stand no sudden
moves enjoy your eggs and shit on shingles

one day I saw three guys share a needle and it was
the best day of their lives at that moment i went
back to reading the Dark Tower and could only
imagine the gunslinger as he peruses the man in
black

CONCERNED

heaven is a crucifix
stares at me from
above the door

my wooden savior stares
into the same void as
you and
Me
there
My
halo
dances

casting
shadows

across
my soul's

widow's
peak

there
has
never

been

any
money

only

soul

soul
is
where

It's
At..

ONLY A LITTLE TIME

to wait
to break a heart
for stars cast down on mountains cover your drying
eyes as you love yourself and say nothing we watch
clouds roll in and laugh smug like cotton dreams

life is easier now in rear view mirrors tears never
matter to those less attuned God only knows to see
us all different as "he" never talks about you in the
spur of the moment

suspended in a masquerade of flesh and bone....

Freedom
only
exists
in the
mind

myth
is
better

than
the
reward

America
is.

built on
Shit
credit
insurance
liabilities
the future
bi
partisan
Rome
horse
In
Congress
fiat money
striped
backs
of the
poor

sweat
on brow
now
Is
sooner
than you expected
wanting
to uphold
the justice
of a
different
regime

ENRAPTURED

lone tears after midnight
staining cosmic satin
where two or more gather
at your tombstone is where
you'll find the mercy seat
it is where you will find
god's reflection
sharpening ideals out of plague and solitude
my sorrow taught me to recognize joy
I've learned that sharpening my axe in
the summer afternoon lessened the impact
of any good words turned to stone
for cherubs to rub on wings before
going into the light
tears will salt the earth barren

THIGHS

smooth glass
even with her
thighs closed
she was beautiful
mystery unfolded
tulip between my fingertips
kissing lips
understand this shakedown
after burning

kindled madness
long way away
pins and needles
hot breath below

PARADISE REEKS

wounds wide open
ghost lost willows
my muse
months ago
turned different shades of grey
never came down this way again to sacrifice
tomb heart torn open after three days in earth
Alone now on Penn Avenue choking on fumes
drunk on deities blood and soul sun follows
reckless gallows shared warmth on my shadow
stone face looking forward to meeting my retreat
impossible
my
loyal soul keeps
coming back
after a long time
away awake
to sleep for once
a long time gone
can smell other dowries paid
blood and money creates extra deities
on her skin where my smell used to lay

beside burning pillows hearts of fire
ablaze as I'm washed out with soot
high hopes still walking up hill
moon following to sacrifices creating mountains
ready to fall on my head going back down is chaos
walking too far past paradise

willows you seek are golden in the sun at dusk
the trick is to be able to look into her smile across
bellies of wheat again leaving the wound that is a
heart wide open

LAY

nude in bed
sunshine awaits
she is religion
high priestess worship
at altar kiss gently

mold her she responds back with gentle pushes
clean leans against me with tenderness

in mind a social identity unchained never stumbles
strong in mind sorry for being loud the end i know
it well... hear her moan behind clouds that float
empty space between the moon

i eat for the winter to come keep belly full warmth
is wholesome warmth is fine a fire from within that
burns this way from a heartbeat that is at peace with
her heart

unleash hell i am her wolf that prays towards
moons to make well trouble already dead she is

solid rock my mountain that burns fires fit for
sacrifice
as she wears me like a ring and i am finally worn
well as i stare into starry eyes

AWAKEN

breeze on lips tingle
a little bit while warm inside
relish these moments of silence
as beasts lie dormant monsters
need
and want
loins ache
rub scent
on her

feel me tomorrow
angels linger on pillows and skin

her love was like ashing a cigarette
from a backseat window

wanted to be stable for a minute
hover around the look she gave me
told her to sit like ancient ivy
we smell like lust

wait for her to dance

a sad beautiful soul
i need
sidecar
a motorcycle
helmet and goggles
rimfire rifle
need to survive
need to kill to eat to fuck to do whatever she wants
recharge batteries
bad brains
tattoos on both wrists

do not feel alone
every stride into the void
everywhere is desolation and triumph
face of everyone who can stand looking into the
bony visage of strangers

those that need you most will roll bones through
curses and cries of languish
only give you money for gasoline or broken teeth

It

starts
to rain

on
my
sad

eerily
beautiful
soul

recognizes
the
difference

the mist

your
tears
on
my
shoulder

will
always
remember
your
words

always
said
i would

GALLOWS

blood on the trail
hanging road
old decay
mojo
hand
points away
from salvation
Laying on my side

struggling
makes you stronger
knuckle
tattoos warning
one look leans
cigarette
burns

an ashtray
survives
she said no thanks man
already burned this town down

Winter Sun
cold as a new marble
awaken from dreams
tossing and turning
in the night

her face written in clouds
fresh morning dew
her smell always on the wind
hot breath on neck
a new
nightmare

since
i
left

my
voice
is softer

except when
in the presence
of the moon

i
howl
for her
memory

scent
touch
close
to me

i
remember
always walk

in the street
Pittsburgh
streets are
made from
crushed
beer cans
buses run flat
Never
willows looking
over

a shoulder
your
robots

will

always rebel
Weight of Love
crush me without
warning.

forgive
tidying
cob
webs
catching
dreams
time
to
believe
belt buckle
impression
inside
her thigh

spirits
smoking
waiting
fires lit
smoke
waiting
gallows

If you want me, you know where to find me for I
am in your heart, to stroke and stoke your soul on
ancient sacred ground, the shadow where angels
fear to tread. I am the streets where junkies lay
down to take last breathes, gasps of pure ecstasy.
Grisly gnarled strangers await death patiently to
steal love as love waits for no one especially not
this morning of fire. She is the cold ground, I am
the fire within everyone who talks of youth odious
death paternal cold grip like a lovers embrace for
the last time and once again like mud in a river as
I'm still here to always find truth in belief but never
in words, actions are truly life's currency that we
exchange for a minute or two as dreams are caught
in Spiderwebs over my bed.

Angel, Fuck, and Payphones & Quarters previously appeared in the Dope Fiend Daily

In Remembrance, My Muse, and Hunger appeared in the Rye Whiskey Review

Burnt Sage Again appeared in the Pangolin Review

Alien Buddha Zine #2

Also Featuring:

"Soulmates" a story from Kevin Tosca

Flash Fiction from Tom Blessing

Poetry from Carl Kaucher, Lee Ballentine, Tom Orbzut, & Kevin Ridgeway

Art from Nikki Knight & Christine Tabaka

Alien Buddha Press 2019

ALIEN BUDDHA ZINE #2

INTERVIEW WITH ADAM LEVON BROWN OF MADNESS MUSE PRESS PG 100

AND MORE!

FICTION FROM ROBERT RAGAN, HEATH BROUGHER, AND RED FOCKS

Art by Marcel Herms, Mike Fiorito, Chandor Gloomy and Ammi Romero

POETRY FROM

Where in the World is the Alien Buddha?

Ammi Romero (Mexico & USA)
R. Keith (Canada)
Olivier Schopfer (Switzerland)
Andrew Darlington (The U.K)
Gideon Cecil (Guyana)
Partha Chatterjee (India)
Vatsala Radhakeesoon (Mauritius)
Marcel Herms (Netherlands)
Billy T Antonio (Philippines)
John Doyle (Ireland)
Don Beukes (France & South Africa)
Elancharan Gunasekaran (Singapore)
Volodymyr Bilyk (Ukraine)
Norbert Góra (Poland)
Bill Lambdin (Finland)
Bengt O Björklund (Sweden)
Kevin Berg (Thailand)
Sudeep Adhikari (Nepal)
Lucia Orellana-Damacela (Ecuador)

Alien Buddha Press 2019

WHERE IN THE WORLD IS
The Alien Buddha?

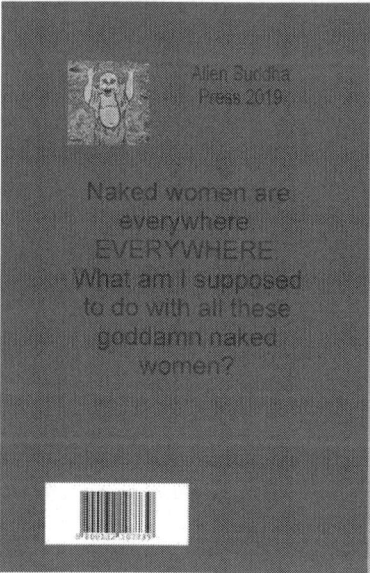
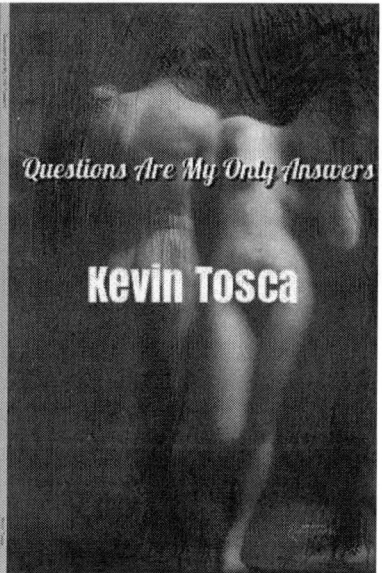

THIS ONE TIME, THE ALIEN BUDDHA
GOT SO HIGH...

ISBN: 9781792052637

A falling moon. A hidden city. And one of you is under attack, an attack that must lead to terminal personality disintegration. In your deep subconscious are a thousand predecessor implants, and implants within those implants. Only one of them knows the reason for the attack... and how it can be stopped...

Part retro-Weird Tales, part Classic SF, all Slipstream Sense of Wonder, this novel takes you down through the DNA core of being, and out beyond forever's farthest star

In the Time of the Breaking

Andrew Darlington

IN THE TIME OF THE BREAKING
NEW DIRECTIONS IN SCIENTIFICTION

Andrew Darlington

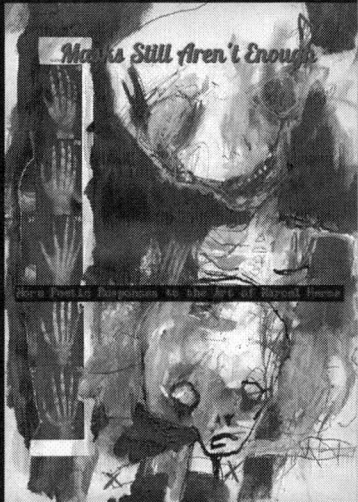

THE PHILANTHROPIST'S SUICIDE

RED FOCKS

R. Keith, Mark Hartenbach, Kevin Ridgeway,
Gabriel Ricard, Thaïs Anne, Luke Kuzmish,
Jeff Weddle, Jason Baldinger, Mark Borczon,
Ryan Quinn Flanagan, Robert JW., Jay Passer,
Stefin Bohdan, Thomas R. Thomas,
Richard J Cronberg, Clinton J Ruston,
John Grochalski, Nathan Tompkins,
Chani Zwibel, Scott Thomas Outlar,
R. Bremner, John Patrick Robbins,
Carl Kaucher, Chelsea Bargeron, Marcel Herms,
and Ammi Romero

Alien Buddha Press 2018

Alien Buddha Press

Alien
Buddha Press
Poetry Anthology #5

Barcode Area
We will add the barcode for you.
Made with Cover Creator

157

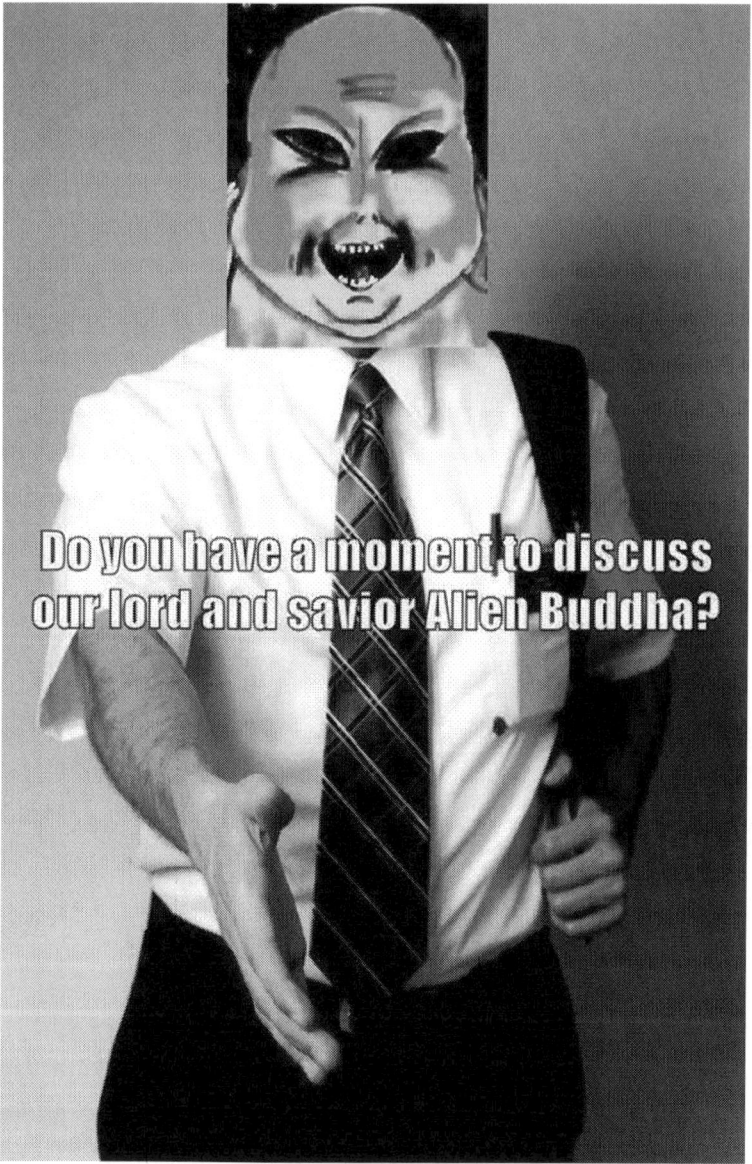

Made in the USA
Middletown, DE
20 March 2019